A Journey With Jesus

40 Day devotional

Andy Brown

Contents

Acknowledgements

With thanks first and foremost to Jesus Christ, my Lord and Saviour, to my darling wife for her wonderful illustration of the Wilderness Cross throughout this book, and to the fellowship of believers at Bramerton Road Community Church which I called home for many years.

Without you, this devotional would never have happened.

Thank you.

Introduction

Welcome to this 40-day devotional booklet which was originally written as a Lent course for Bramerton Road Community Church. It can be read over any forty day period, and doesn't have to be read over Lent. Each day shouldn't take more than a couple of minutes to read. Each day is made up of a verse from the Bible, a short reading, a prayer, a few questions to think on or discuss, and finally a word of encouragement.

I hope that you will enjoy reading this, and that God will use it to speak to you in many ways. I pray that these words will both challenge and encourage you, and most importantly, that you will draw nearer to God.

Bless you in Jesus' name.
Andy Brown

Day 1 - The Journey Begins...

"Then Jesus was led by the Spirit into the desert to be tempted by the devil. After fasting forty days and forty nights, he was hungry." - Matthew 4:1-2 (NIV)

The Bible tells us that Jesus spent forty days and forty nights in the desert, being tested by the devil. This happened before Jesus entered His ministry, and I've often wondered what He spent His days doing. It is clear that He was preparing for the ministry He would conduct, which would ultimately lead to the cross, but what did He spend time thinking about? Well, the Bible doesn't tell us exactly, but it is possible, I believe, He would have thought about the following:

- How much His Father loved Him
- Who He was
- The things He would need to do to stay strong
- What He would teach the people
- Resisting the devil's attacks
- What His ministry would look like

And these are the things that we are going to think about over the next forty days. They are very important, and will have a positive impact on your relationship with God.

Our verse for today ends by saying "He was hungry," - what an understatement! If I hadn't eaten for forty days or nights, I'd be more than just "hungry!" The first time I fasted, I thought I was doing great until I looked at the clock and realised I'd only been going 45 minutes!

While you may not be hungry for food at the end of this journey, it is my keen hope and prayer that you will be ever so hungry for more of God. There is so much He wants to do in your life, and I believe you'll see a glimpse of that in the coming days. Tomorrow, we'll begin to think about God's love for you, because that is the foundation of everything.

Prayer
Lord, over the coming days, I pray that You will speak to me. I ask You to draw me closer to You, and to teach me the things you want me to know. Amen.

Questions to ponder or discuss:
- What do you hope God will do for you over the next forty days?
- Jesus set aside a long time to be with God, how hard is it to set aside even a small amount of time to be with Him each day?
- What can you do to ensure you get the most out of this journey you can?

A Word of Encouragement – *No matter where you are in your journey with God, He is always wanting to share more with you. Today is the first day of a new journey with the Father.*

Part 1 – God's Love for you

Day 2 - God Chose You

"We know, dear brothers and sisters, that God loves you and has chosen you to be his own people." - 1 Thessalonians 1:4 (NLT)

God chose you. He chose you to be His very own.

It was not an accident, but a deliberate act of His will. Out of all of the people God has created, He specifically chose you to be in His family forever. That should make you feel pretty special!

We don't always think very highly of ourselves. In fact, it's often hard to find anyone who actually likes themselves all that much. But God, in His infinite wisdom, selected you, because He thinks you're amazing. It's hard for us to believe that such an amazing and awesome God could even be interested in us, let alone pick us out. But that's exactly what He's done.

It's not an accident either, that you find yourself in the church or community that you are in. Not only did God choose you, but He has placed you in that community to fulfil His will and purpose for your life. God has put you there because He knows that He can bless you by being there, and secondly use you in His service.

Where you live may not be the most glamorous of places. It may not be Paris or New York, or even London. But, it is a real place; a real corner of the world where God is working. God wants to bring His kingdom – His way of being and doing right – to your community. He can only do that through us – the family of believers. And importantly, He can only do that if we realise that we are here for that very purpose.

God loves you more than you can imagine. He thinks about you all of the time, and is willing to stop and listen whenever you want to talk. Would you do anything less for your own children? Only when we realise how special we are to God, can we really embrace our place in His family and the role He has given to us.

Spend some time today thinking about how special you are to God.

Prayer

Father, You have chosen me for Your family. It's sometimes hard for me to accept and to understand that, but please help me grasp it. Tell me today how much You love me, and root me in that love. In Jesus' name, Amen

Questions to ponder or discuss:
- Does it make you feel special to know that God chose you to be part of His family?
- Why do we find it easier to believe that God loves others more than us?
- Why do you think God has placed you in the church or community you are in?

A Word of Encouragement – *Often people will let us down, hurt us or reject us. However, God will never, ever let us down, or reject us from His family. He loves you as you are, warts and all!*

Day 3 - No Surprises

"I make known the end from the beginning, from ancient times, what is still to come. I say: My purpose will stand, and I will do all that I please." - Isaiah 46:10 (NIV)

God knows the end from the beginning. Before He starts anything, He already knows how it's going to finish. I bet there are times in your life that you wished you had known the end of a thing, before you started it!

God, being omnipotent (meaning infinite in power) and omnipresent (meaning present at all places all of the time), is rather difficult to surprise! You can't sneak up on God, or make Him jump. You can't shock Him, nor can you do anything that He doesn't see coming. You are no surprise to God.

Yesterday we learned that God specifically chose us to be His own. That is even more spectacular when you realise that God knows your darkest secrets, that He knows every mistake you're going to make and that He knows every sin you are going to commit. Knowing all of that, God still chose you!

Sometimes when we get it wrong and do something we know God is not pleased with, we draw back and think God is angry with us. We humanise Him and think He'll act like we do – getting cross or refusing to speak to us. But He doesn't. When we get it wrong, Father is not up in heaven shaking His head saying, "Jesus, did you see what they just did? I can't believe it! I never saw that coming!" God will never be pleased with our bad behaviour, but He will never reject us for it either. He wants to be in relationship with us.

Many people have said to me, "I'm not good enough to go to church." While they may feel this way, it is completely wrong. None of us are good enough to approach God, but that's why He sent His Son Jesus to make a way for us. The church is full of people who need Jesus – we all do!

God knows you intimately. He knows your best and your worst. None of those things make Him love you any more or any less. Remember, you are no surprise to God!

Prayer
We thank You Father for loving us so much that You will never reject us. Even though You know each and every mistake we will ever make, You still made a way for us through Your Son. Thank You, and help us remember we don't surprise You. Amen.

Questions to ponder or discuss:
- When you make a mistake, do you draw back from God?
- Does it comfort you to know that God has already seen your mistakes, and still loves you?
- How can you share God's love in your community?

A Word of Encouragement – *God is not surprised by you or your behaviour. Rejoice in the freedom that gives you today.*

Day 4 - Nothing Can Separate Us

"No power in the sky above or in the earth below—indeed, nothing in all creation will ever be able to separate us from the love of God that is revealed in Christ Jesus our Lord." - Romans 8:39 (NLT)

If you have children, then you've probably experienced that heart-stopping time when you turned around and they were not there. Perhaps you were in a shop, or just walking down the road, but for a few dreadful seconds, you were separated from them. If you don't have children, I'm sure you can imagine the sudden panic and cold sweat you must momentarily feel.

Why do we have such feelings? The answer is simple – because we love our children, and the thought of losing them is terrifying!

God tells us in His Word that nothing can separate us from His love. Nothing in the sky, nothing on earth, and nothing in the sea. Not one single thing will ever be able to come between you and God's love.

The verse today is meant for you. Sometimes we read the Bible and nod along in agreement with it, but don't really accept the truth that it was meant for us. When God created His Word, He had you in mind. He knew that you would be reading this verse today, and He wanted you to know that He loves you. It is not just a nice statement or sound bite, but a real message for you – *nothing* can separate you from God's love.

Let me ask you – what could your children do that would make you stop loving them? It is probably not an answer that comes easily to you, and you would need a lot of time to think it over. Your answer, in all likelihood, will be – nothing. There isn't anything they could do that would make us stop loving them – "They're our kids!" God thinks the same about us. There isn't anything you can do that would make Him stop loving you – no mistake, no sin, no failure – nothing. That's an amazing truth.

Prayer
Heavenly Father, thank You so much that Your love is so strong, that nothing can ever separate us from You. We thank You for the safety that gives us. Amen

Questions to ponder or discuss:
- Do you ever feel like there are things that divide you from God?
- Does it make you feel secure to know that there is nothing that can separate you from God?
- Do we ever take God's love for granted?

A Word of Encouragement – *No matter what your past is, or what mistakes you are making right now, God loves you. You can feel safe, knowing that nothing can separate you from His love.*

Day 5 - God Sent His Son

"For God so loved the world that he gave his one and only Son, that whoever believes in him shall not perish but have eternal life." - John 3:16 (NIV)

Before Martha (our daughter) was born, I couldn't imagine what it would be like to be a dad. Now that she's here, I couldn't imagine being without her! What would I give her up for? Absolutely nothing at all. What could there be that is important enough that it would make me give up someone so precious?

God feels the same way about His own Son, but yet He answers the question differently. The one thing that He would give up His Son for – is you.

God loves you so much, that He was willing to give up His one and only Son in order that you might live. He gave up the most precious thing, because He knew it was the only way He could bring you back to Him. That should make you feel pretty special. God sowed a Son to gain a family.

Salvation was the hardest thing God ever had to do. It was so difficult, because it cost Him so much. Jesus isn't just God's Son, but He is part of God Himself. We can't begin to understand how hard it was for God to separate Himself from His Son for the time He was on the Earth. Yet He did all of that, and more, because He loved us so deeply.

What is the most precious thing in your life? How much would you have to love someone, in order to give that thing up for them? Please don't underestimate how hard it was for God. The next time you find yourself doubting God's love for you, just remember what He had to give up in order to save you.

Giving is an expression of love. We see in our verse for today that God so loved, that He *gave*. We give to those we love, whether it's money, time, effort, forgiveness, help, encouragement or any other thing. One way of expressing love is by giving gifts. The greatest gift God is giving you today is His love. Gifts however, to be enjoyed, must first be opened. Open God's gift today, and receive His love by thinking about His Son.

Prayer

Father, we know that the hardest thing You have ever done is give up Your Son for us. We cannot thank You enough for this amazing gift. Please help us to remember Your Son, and the death He died on our behalf. In Jesus' name, Amen

Questions to ponder or discuss:
- What is your most prized possession, and who would you be willing to give it up to?
- What can you do to accept God's love in a deeper way today?
- Do you find it hard to believe that God would do this for you? Why? What can you do about that?

A Word of Encouragement – *God has given you everything He has.*

Day 6 - God Knows Your Name

"But now, O Jacob, listen to the Lord who created you. O Israel, the one who formed you says, "Do not be afraid, for I have ransomed you. *I have called you by name; you are mine.* " - Isaiah 43:1 (NLT) *underline added*

I once heard a story about a woman named Christine; an evangelist with a large ministry. When she was in her thirties, she received a letter from the government that informed her she was adopted. Her parents had never told her. The paperwork not only described her as "unwanted" but it also said she was "unnamed". Not only had Christine's birth mother given her up, but she had not even given her a name. Imagine that, not just being unwanted but also having no name. It must have been devastating to discover.

I don't know what kind of upbringing you had; whether you had a happy childhood – perhaps you were adopted yourself. Whatever your background, if you ever felt "unnamed," I've got some good news for you today.

You're probably not a famous person, or even that well known. You may live in a small town, and feel that it is somewhere that no one has ever heard of. All in all, you may feel pretty insignificant sometimes. I want you to know that this is not the case at all. God knows your name!

No matter how unknown you may feel, God knows exactly who you are. He has called you by your name. He created you specifically, and it was no accident. God knew what He was doing when He made you. Not only that, but He has placed you in your church, family and community for a reason.

God wants you to be part of His church, and has put you where you are so that you can contribute what only you can bring. God knows your name, and He knows your strengths and your gifts. Without you, the church would not be complete.

You are valuable, and your contribution – no matter how small you think it is – is not going unnoticed. Even if you feel somewhat unappreciated, God appreciates you. What more appreciation do we need?

Prayer
Lord God, we thank You so much that not only do You know our name,
but You have called us by it. Thank You for placing us where we are,
and for the contribution we can make to Your Kingdom. In Jesus'
name, Amen

Questions to ponder or discuss:
- How does it make you feel to know that God knows your name?
- Did you realise that you are an important part of your church?
- How can you encourage someone in the church family who feels
insignificant or unappreciated?

A Word of Encouragement – *God knows exactly who you are – you're*
famous in heaven!

Part 2 – Who we are in Christ

your name is Precious One.

Day 7 - Brand New

"Therefore, if anyone is in Christ, he is a new creation; the old has gone, the new has come!" - 2 Corinthians 5:17 (NIV)

Don't you just love new things? Isn't it an exciting time when you get a new house, and isn't it great to show off a brand new car or outfit you've just bought? New things feel fresh and clean, and are often far superior to the old things that they replace. I don't know if you realise it, but when you accepted Jesus as your Saviour and Lord, you became brand new.

You've probably heard the expression "born again." This comes from the fact that when we become Christians, God completely renews us. He takes us, in whatever state we are in, and totally refreshes our spirits. You might be thinking, "I don't feel that fresh and new!"

The truth is that although God makes our spirits brand new, it can often take a lot of time for that newness to come through into our lives. The new spirit has to overcome the old "flesh," or "sinful nature" which we have picked up over time, living in the world and being apart from God. One of the aims of our Christian life is to bring forth that new nature of ours into our everyday lives.

What is this new nature like, you might ask. Well, that's what we're going to learn over the next few days. It is vitally important that you realise who you are in Christ. You must learn what your new nature is like, so that you can develop it. These are not things that you will be, or even things that you could be, but rather these are things you *are* – right now! God has made it so.

Some of the things that you learn about yourself may not be that familiar, and you may not recognise them in yourself. But let me assure you, every one of them is stated very clearly in God's Word, and if it says it there, it must be true!

Knowing who you really are is supremely important. It will change your life, and how you look at yourself.

Prayer

Heavenly Father, in the next few days we're going to be learning about our new nature in Christ. Please help us to understand who we are, and what You have done for us. In Jesus' name, Amen

Questions to ponder or discuss:
- When you became a Christian, was there anything suddenly or dramatically different about you (as that can sometimes happen)?
- Is it hard to accept that we change inside when we become Christians?

A Word of Encouragement – *You may not be where you want to be in life, but look back – you've probably come a long way! Rejoice in the new start God has given you.*

2020
New Year. New start. New decade.

Day 8 - Sainthood

"Paul, an apostle of Christ Jesus by the will of God, To the saints in Ephesus, the faithful in Christ Jesus:" - Ephesians 1:1 (NIV)

If I asked you to picture a "saint" in your mind, what would you think of? Probably a particularly holy or gentle person; a person who gives up their life for others in good works. In the Roman Catholic Church, certain people are recognised as saints (it's called being canonised) when they have lived a very special life of goodness and humility, and have performed some kind of miracle.

The truth however, according to God's Word, is rather different. It actually says that *you* are a saint – a holy one. Paul wrote to the church at Ephesus (and others), and always addressed it to the "saints" or to the "holy, consecrated people" . Paul was writing to churches just like yours – he was writing to people like you and me.

It may be a bit of a shock to you to find out that you're a saint, but believe me, you are. The next time you go to church, I want you to have a look around. All of those people around you are saints too. Sainthood is not a matter of performance, but rather one of *position* - a position that God has blessed us with.

You are no longer a "sinner" anymore, but a saint who sometimes sins. Being a saint doesn't mean you get everything right all the time, far from it, but it does mean you have a pure spirit, and have been set aside for God. While you may not feel pure on the outside, your heart has been washed clean in the blood of Jesus, making it as pure as He is.

I hope that the realisation that you are a saint will make you look at yourself differently. When you look in the mirror, don't see yourself as a broken sinner (or however you may see yourself) but as a pure-hearted, consecrated man or woman of God. That should give you confidence and hope.

According to the Bible, you are Saint <insert name here> !

Susan Sumption

Prayer

Thank You Lord for making me a saint, and for washing me in Your precious blood. I am now holy and pure, and ready to serve You. In Jesus' name, Amen.

Questions to ponder or discuss:
- How do you feel about being a saint?
- Does being a saint make you see yourself in a different way?
- Is it hard to accept the fact that you are holy? Why?

A Word of Encouragement – *Think about the people you might see today – you could be the only saint they meet. Make sure you bless them!*

Day 9 - Forgiven

"In Whom we have our redemption through His blood, [which means] the forgiveness of our sins." - Colossians 1:14 (Amp)

One of the worst feelings a person can experience is the weight of guilt. It feels like a heavy chain around our necks, and casts a dark shadow over everything we do. Have you ever seen a film version of a "Christmas Carol"? There's a scene where Jacob Marley returns to warn Scrooge about his wicked ways. Often Marley's ghost is depicted being covered in heavy, metal chains. This is exactly how feelings of guilt and shame can feel to us – every day!

If you think back over your life, you can probably think of many examples where you've made mistakes, or worse, done things deliberately that you're not proud of. Perhaps sometimes you sit in church and look around, thinking that the other people around you are much "holier" than you are. We've all done it.

The truth is that we have all missed the mark. God's perfect standards are beyond our reach, and on our own, we can never grasp them. It doesn't matter how close we get, if we fall short, we fall short. It's like jumping over a bottomless chasm – if you miss the edge by a mile, you will fall; if you miss it by one inch, you will still fall.

If you're like me, then sometimes you will feel that you're not good enough and that you don't deserve God's grace. But, that's what makes grace so good! We don't deserve it!

You are forgiven. The verse above tells you plainly that by being washed in Jesus' blood, you are forgiven – once and for all. When were you forgiven? The first time you asked Him. Forgiveness is freely offered by God, and it is yours from the very second you accept Christ as your Saviour.

If you've been carrying round a heavy weight of guilt and shame, then I strongly urge you to get before God and receive His forgiveness. All you have to do is ask! The great thing is, if you've already asked, then it is yours! You are forgiven – redeemed – now and for ever more!

Prayer

Lord, it is a wonder that you can forgive us for the things that we have done. But we rejoice in that truth, and thank You so much for sending Jesus to set us free! Amen

Questions to ponder or discuss:
- Why do we find it hard to accept God's forgiveness?
- Some say they don't *feel* forgiven, does that matter?
- Does knowing that you're forgiven make you feel free?

A Word of Encouragement – *God has removed your sins from you as far as the east is from the west – that's pretty far!*

Day 10 - Sons of God

"For in Christ Jesus you are all sons of God through faith." - Galatians 3:26 (Amp)

In our politically correct world, we often translate Bible verses (such as the one above) in such a way as to say "children" rather than "sons". But by doing so, we can often miss the point.

The son, especially in the biblical culture, was a very important part of a family. And whether it is right or not, the son was given a higher place than a daughter. The son, and especially the first born, was the one who was entitled to the biggest share of the inheritance, was the one who had the highest rank and place in the family, and was the one who was the most honoured among his brothers and sisters.

That's the position that God has given to you. You do not just have the position of God's child, as great as that may be, but you have been given the place of a *son*. This means you are entitled to the first place in the family, to the honour and to the inheritance. This is not a position you have earned, or even a position that you have been given based on your performance or talent. Rather, this is a position you have been given because God loves you so very much.

In our culture today, we don't tend to value a son over a daughter. We love our children, and in the UK at least, we don't tend to think of one sex as being superior to another. But whether you are blessed with a son or a daughter, what would you give for them? What would you do for them if you could? Most of us would give anything and everything we could for the sake of our children.

Often parents take out life insurance and all kinds of financial plans so that they can provide for their children. A parent will go without, in order that their child may have some kind of blessing. Who of us, if our children came to us asking for help or to meet a need, wouldn't do absolutely everything we could to give it to them? God is the same way in treating us.

Enjoy your position as not only a child, but a *son* of God.

Prayer
Lord Jesus, You are the Father's true and firstborn Son, and yet You, through Your blood, have given us the position of sonship. We thank You for that glorious blessing. In Jesus' name, Amen

Questions to ponder or discuss:
- If you have children, is there anything you wouldn't do for them?
- How do you feel about having the position of a "son" in God's family?
- As parents, how would we want our children to approach us? Would God be different?

A Word of Encouragement – *Don't forget the wonderful position that God has given you, and don't be afraid to approach Him today – He loves to hear your voice.*

Day 11 - Citizens of Heaven

"But our citizenship is in heaven. And we eagerly await a Saviour from there, the Lord Jesus Christ," - Philippians 3:20 (NIV)

Have you ever felt out of place in the world? Like, for whatever reason, you just didn't fit in with everyone else. The reason is simple – you don't belong to this world! Our verse for today tells us very clearly that we are not part of this world, but are rather citizens of heaven.

If someone asked you where you live, what would you say? The name of your street? Or perhaps you might give the name of your town or city. Maybe, depending on the circumstances, you might say "England," or even "The United Kingdom," (if you're from there!) While these are all valid places, they are not strictly the truth.

We are spiritual beings, like God, but we live in a physical body. That body may be set firmly on the Earth, but our spiritual "home" is in heaven.

Citizenship is an important concept. If you are born in a country, then usually you automatically become a citizen. However, if you want to become a citizen of a country you were not born in, then you have to go through a great deal to earn it. You might need to learn a lot of detailed information about that country, and even take a test to demonstrate your knowledge. Heaven's citizenship test however, is rather simpler. Do you believe and accept Jesus Christ as Lord and Saviour?

If you believe in Jesus, and what He did at the cross, then you are a citizen of heaven. You don't have to worry about belonging any longer, because you now belong to God and are part of His family. Your heavenly citizenship cannot be revoked and is not given under condition. Once you're in, you're in!

While God certainly wants you to enjoy your life here on Earth, He also wants you to remember that you're not home yet. And when you get there, He's going to throw the biggest party you could imagine!

Prayer

Father, thank You that we have our home waiting for us in Heaven. Thank You for blessing us with eternal citizenship in Your Kingdom. Help us to remember where we truly belong. In Jesus' name. Amen

Questions to ponder or discuss:
- Have you ever felt like you didn't belong? What was it like?
- Is it good to know that your real home is in heaven?
- What do you think it will be like to take up your citizenship in heaven?

A Word of Encouragement – *If you ever feel like you don't belong, then remember where your true home is.*

Day 12 - Blessed in the heavenlies

"Praise be to the God and Father of our Lord Jesus Christ, who has blessed us in the heavenly realms with every spiritual blessing in Christ." - Ephesians 1:3 (NIV)

We have been thinking about who we are in Christ – the position we are given once we are born again. Today, I want to talk about the blessing granted to us by God.

Before we go any further, please read the verse above once again. What tense is it written in? Present tense? Future tense? No, it is written in past tense. Paul, who wrote this letter, is clearly telling us that the blessing of God is something we already have. It isn't something we are going to get in the future, nor is it something we're receiving now. The blessing of God is ours, and has been since we gave our lives to Jesus.

Many Christians spend their lives trying to get God to bless them. They think if they can work hard enough, or behave well enough, that God might just give them the things that they desire. This is deception, and if this is how you've been living, it's time to stop. God has blessed us – **_has_** – it is already ours.

What has He blessed us with exactly? With every blessing in the heavenly realms. Not some blessings, or many blessings, but every single blessing available in the heavenly places. That is a lot of blessing!

The rest of Ephesians 1 (up to verse 14), goes on to talk about some of these blessings that you and I have been given by God in Christ. These blessings aren't just for the super-apostles (Paul, Peter etc.) but also for us too.

The blessing includes God choosing us for His very own, and for Him adopting us as sons into His family. Remember, being a son isn't a male thing, but rather a positional thing. Sons, in the biblical culture, had the first rights of the inheritance of the Father.

As well as adoption, the blessing includes redemption through the blood of Jesus and the forgiveness of sins (v7). Redemption means rescue – it means that God has paid the price for us and our sins are no more. What a thing to be thankful for.

Remember, the blessing is already yours! Spend some time today thanking God for it.

Prayer

Father, what can we say? You have blessed us with every blessing – with everything You have – so we thank You in the precious name of Jesus. Amen

Questions to ponder or discuss:
- Is it hard for you to believe that you have been blessed?
- Do you sometimes find yourself trying to earn God's blessing?
- If you have time, read through Ephesians 1:3-14 and meditate on the blessings you have. Which ones are you most thankful for?

A Word of Encouragement – *Don't try to earn God's blessing, it's already yours!*

Part 3 – Staying Strong in the Lord

Day 13 - True Worship

"Yet a time is coming and has now come when the true worshipers will worship the Father in spirit and truth, for they are the kind of worshipers the Father seeks." - John 4:23 (NIV)

Worship should be a way of life. It is not an activity we perform once a week on a Sunday, nor is it a simple act of singing songs (although music can be a vehicle for worship). Worship should be as easy and natural to us as breathing is, and when it is, it helps us to stay strong in the Lord.

Our verse for today may well be familiar to you, but I heard something recently that I want to share with you. We often say that we want to be a people who worship the Father in spirit and in truth, but that's not what the verse says. It says that the Father desires *worshippers* who worship Him in spirit and truth. This is an important distinction.

There is a huge difference between being someone who worships God, and someone who is a worshipper. A worshipper is someone who naturally and freely worships God, and is strengthened by their close and intimate relationship with Him.

1 Corinthians 14:26 says that "...When you come together, everyone has a hymn, or a word of instruction, a revelation, a tongue or an interpretation. All of these must be done for the strengthening of the church." All these different aspects of a service are forms of worship, and these things not only give glory to God, but also strengthen the church. If we want to be strong, we need to learn to worship God continually.

To worship in spirit means to worship God on His level. For instance, we can sing songs as an outward sign of worship, but our hearts and minds are focussed on anything other than God. Worshipping in spirit, is a spiritual act, and can be done anywhere and anytime.

To worship in truth means to worship God for who He is, and not for who we think He is or we want Him to be. Worshipping in truth means coming to God in honesty, presenting ourselves as we are – not hiding or pretending we're something that we're not.

True worship is a lifestyle that makes us strong!

Prayer
Father, we want to worship You for who You are, not for who we think You are. Help our worship to be pleasing to You, and to be in spirit and in truth. In Jesus' name, Amen

Questions to ponder or discuss:
- What does "worship" mean to you?
- In tough times, does it make you feel better when you worship God?
- Do you find it difficult to focus when worshipping, and stopping your mind from wandering?

A Word of Encouragement – *Worship God today in all that you do; whether it's washing up or working. God is always with you.*

Day 14 - Prayer Power

"Confess your sins to each other and pray for each other so that you may be healed. The earnest prayer of a righteous person has great power and produces wonderful results." - James 5:16 (NLT)

While looking at our position in Christ earlier in this book, one of the things we could have learned is that we (Christians that is) are the righteousness of God in Christ. 2 Corinthians 5:21 says "God made him who had no sin to be sin for us, so that in him we might become the righteousness of God." If you combine this amazing truth with our verse for today, you see that our prayers are powerful weapons with wonderful results.

We are righteous because of what Jesus did for us on the cross, and our prayers are powerful because of who we pray to – God. When we pray, we allow God to work in the world. Our prayers release the power of God into any situation that we pray for. If we want to stay strong in the Lord, we need to learn to not just pray regularly, but to live a life of prayer.

So often in the Gospels, we read of Jesus going off somewhere to pray. We hear many accounts where He prays for people, and times of praise and worship of His Father. This close intimacy with God, made (and kept) Jesus strong for the many trials He faced. We, even more so, need the power and strength of God to work in our lives. We cannot get away with not praying.

Prayer can become a chore when we view it as just another religious activity that we're *supposed* to be doing. Like many, you have probably felt guilty for not praying enough. The purpose of today's devotional is not to condemn you even more! In fact, the opposite is true, I want this to free you.

Prayer keeps us strong. It allows God to work in our lives and the lives of those we pray for. It maintains our relationship with God, which is critical. We can't expect to see God working in our lives if we don't ask Him to get involved. We can't live a life that pleases Him, unless we spend time listening to what He wants, and discerning His will for us.

Prayer is good for you! Enjoy it, because God does!

Prayer

Father, what an amazing privilege it is to spend time in Your presence each day. Thank You for the wonderful results that prayer produces. In the name of Jesus, Amen

Questions to ponder or discuss:
- Do you find yourself viewing prayer as a chore sometimes?
- Do you find that prayer strengthens you spiritually?
- How do you cope when prayers are not answered in the way you expected?

A Word of Encouragement – *Prayer produces wonderful results, and that's a great reason to start today*

Day 15 - The Living and Active Word

"For the word of God is living and active. Sharper than any double-edged sword, it penetrates even to dividing soul and spirit, joints and marrow; it judges the thoughts and attitudes of the heart." - Hebrews 4:12 (NIV)

You will never be strong in the Lord, unless you feed regularly on His living and active Word. Reading and studying the Bible is like having a spiritual meal, and without it, your spirit will never be fit or healthy. Like your body, your spirit needs to be fed with a healthy diet, and like your body, without regular food, it can become sick and weak – or even die. The good thing is that you can never "overeat" spiritually!

The Word of God that we read in the Bible is not simply a set of instructions recorded on a page. The Scriptures are both living and active. That means they are powerful and relevant in many situations

God's Word is alive and that means we can read a passage one day, and God will speak to us about it. The next day, we could read the very same passage, and God could speak to us in a totally different way. While the words themselves are unchanging, the heart and message behind them can speak in different ways. This is the difference between the Greek words "logos" and "rhema," both translated as "word" in English. *Logos* is the written Word of God, and *rhema* is the "utterance of Christ", or the more personal message meant for you in a particular situation.

One of your pastor's sermons on a Sunday can deliver a hundred different messages (rhema), as each member of the congregation hears distinctly from God. Learning to hear the Lord's message for you is very important. The Bible was written a long time ago and can seemingly bear no relevance to our modern world. However, the Bible is just as relevant today as it ever was. We just need to train our spirits to detect the timeless principle, and apply it to our lives. The *logos* doesn't change, but the *rhema* is new to us each day.

In a world where there is so much uncertainty and falsity, God's Word can be relied on. The Bible is truth. In John 8:32, Jesus tells us that the truth will set us free, but to do so, we must first *know* it! We can only know it by taking time each day to read and study. You will never be who God wants you to be, unless you take His Word seriously.

Prayer
Lord, we thank You for Your living and active Word. May You lead us into all truth, as we spend time each day reading and studying. In Jesus' name, Amen

Questions to ponder or discuss:
- Do you read God's Word because it benefits you, or because you feel obligated to do so?
- How can you make time to read the Bible each day?
- What can you do to ensure your time in the Bible is fresh, and doesn't become dull and stale?

A Word of Encouragement – *Reading and understanding God's Word can be difficult at times, but it is well worth the effort!*

Day 16 - Time Alone with God

"But Jesus often withdrew to lonely places and prayed." - Luke 5:16 (NIV)

Jesus died, not to give you a religion, but to give you a relationship. The relationship He died to give us is a very special one – it is with God Himself. We cannot succeed as Christians unless we put time into that relationship. Time is a precious thing – no matter what you do, you can never earn more of it and you can so easily waste it. Time is the one thing we all have equally, but only some of us use it wisely.

Our relationship with the Father is no different from any other relationship we have. How close would you be to your spouse, children, or friends, if you never spent any time with them? The answer is not close at all. You would be more like acquaintances than intimate children, and Jesus did not suffer as He did just to give us a mediocre acquaintance.

If you want to be a strong and mature Christian, you will have to spend regular time with God. That may mean you have to sacrifice some of the things you would like to do. It may mean turning off the television, or saying no to someone taking you out. However, there is nothing you can give up that is more precious than your time with God.

Jesus, holy and perfect as He was, needed to spend regular time with His Father. He needed to seek His will, gain encouragement and strength, and He needed to have and enjoy fellowship. If Jesus needed to do that, how much more do we need to do it?

There is nothing the devil will fight against harder than your time with God. He will disrupt it in any way that he can, because he knows if you get with God, you will be a threat to him.

When Moses left God's presence, his face shone with glory (Exodus 34:29). We, too, shine in our spirits when we spend time with God. When we go out into the world, we ought to shine with God's power and glory, and point people to Him. Think of yourself as a sort of battery; the more time you spend with God, the more charge you will have, and the stronger you will be to live out a life of love and service in His Name.

Prayer

Father, thank You for the privilege of spending time with You. May You help us to put time with You at the top of our list. In Jesus' name, Amen

Questions to ponder or discuss:
- What things disrupt your time with God? Busyness
- What things can you do when spending time with God? Listern to Him
- How much time do you spend on average fellowshipping with Jesus? Is that enough? It various

A Word of Encouragement – *Spending time with God is essential, but can be very difficult. Don't be discouraged if you struggle – keep trying, it's worth it! God values every single minute you have with Him.*

Day 17 - Fellowship

"And let us not neglect our meeting together, as some people do, but encourage one another, especially now that the day of his return is drawing near." - Hebrews 10:25 (NLT)

The word "fellowship" means a friendly relationship, companionship and a community. It's all about people. The church is made up of people; it's not a building, or an organisation, but a group of individuals following God.

Relationships with people are hard work, and can often be difficult, but human beings were built to be in relationship. God made Adam, but said it wasn't good for him to be alone (Genesis 2:18) – so he made him a companion, Eve. Adam and Eve shared fellowship with one another, as they shared fellowship with God.

I hope that the church where you worship has a wonderful fellowship. One of the best things about the church is the fact that it is built on love. The members should genuinely care about each other, and that is a crucial part of church life.

Fellowship is not just shared on a Sunday morning, when we're all together, but also during the week at various groups. When I think of fellowship, I think about our house group. We vary greatly in age, experience, background, and lifestyle, yet when we meet together we enjoy one another's company. That's the great thing about fellowship – variety.

Variety is a great asset to the church, but can also be a source of problems. We are all different, and one aspect of Christian maturity is learning to rejoice in those differences, and not allowing them to divide us. Some of us can stand up at the front and speak, others find that difficult. Some welcome people on the door, while others prefer to be less visible. The thing is, we all need each other. If even one of us is missing, we all feel it in some way. Of course we would miss the preacher if they didn't show up, but we would also soon notice if the cleaner stopped cleaning, or if no one made the tea after the service.

Fellowship is vital to the ongoing work of the church – we need one another. Some say they can worship God alone, without being part of a church. This may be true to an extent, but we were not made to worship in isolation. We need each other!

Prayer
Lord, we thank You for the fellowship at our church. Help us to do our part to build up the family and keep it healthy and strong. In Jesus' name, Amen

Questions to ponder or discuss:
- What practical things can you do to support the fellowship where you worship?
- What can you do to include those who are unable to attend church on a Sunday?
- How long do you think you could last as a strong Christian, if you were on your own?

A Word of Encouragement – *You are a vital part of the church. Without you, we are incomplete.*

Day 18 - Doing Good

"So let's not get tired of doing what is good. At just the right time we will reap a harvest of blessing if we don't give up." - Galatians 6:9 (NLT)

"If you know these things, blessed and happy and to be envied are you if you practice them [if you act accordingly and really do them]." - John 13:17 (Amp)

If you have been in the world for any length of time, you will know that people often encounter problems. Both in and out of church, I've known people suffering all kinds of situations – financial difficulties, physical and mental health problems, marriage break-ups, and many other tough things. When we face such things, it can be very tempting to lock ourselves away, pray if we're able, and just try to survive in our own way.

I want to share something amazing with you today, and something you may find hard to accept. When we're hurting, the best thing we can do is get out and help someone else. We won't feel like doing it, and it won't be easy, but it will make a difference. Why?

Firstly, helping someone else means they are blessed. Secondly, it gets your mind off of the problem that you are facing. Thirdly, it sows a seed into the Kingdom, and it means you will reap a harvest. Fourthly, it will make you feel better. Fifthly, it will repay the devil back, even in a small way, for what he's putting you through.

Our verse from Galatians today is very clear. It tells us that if we don't get tired of doing good, then we will reap blessings. I believe that doing good to others is one of the most important, yet underdone, things a Christian needs to do to stay strong in the Lord.

Our second verse, from John's Gospel, are some of the final words of Jesus. He says these things just after He has washed His disciples' feet – an act of service. Service means "doing good" to someone. Jesus says quite plainly that if you do these sorts of things (good deeds, acts of service for others) you will be blessed and happy.

Look around your church on a Sunday morning, who do you see that you can do something for? What about your home group, is there someone who needs help in some way? If you look, *really* look, it won't take you long to find someone.

Prayer
Father God, goodness is a fruit of the Spirit, and something we need to practice in our lives. We can often be selfish, so please help us to do good for others. Amen

Questions to ponder or discuss:
- Can you think of three good things to do for people in your life today?
- Do you think that doing good during a time of trial will help you?
- How can you make sure you are a doer of the Word, not just a hearer?

A Word of Encouragement – *God wants to bring a harvest of blessings into your life, give Him an opportunity to do so by sowing some seeds of goodness.*

Day 19 - Peace I leave with you

"Peace I leave with you; My [own] peace I now give and bequeath to you. Not as the world gives do I give to you. Do not let your hearts be troubled, neither let them be afraid. [Stop allowing yourselves to be agitated and disturbed; and do not permit yourselves to be fearful and intimidated and cowardly and unsettled.]" - John 14:27 (Amp)

Have you written a will? A strange or even morbid question, you might think, but an important one. If you do have one, what kind of things are you leaving to your family or friends? Junk? Old rubbish? Worn out or useless items you don't want anymore? No, of course not, you're likely leaving things of value – be it financial or sentimental.

Jesus is no different. In today's verse, we read that Jesus has "bequeathed" peace to us. To bequeath, means to leave to someone in a will. Jesus hasn't left us something old or worn out, but something vitally important and precious – His peace.

Peace is incredibly important if you want to stay strong in the Lord. So many people, both in and out of church, are disturbed and distressed most of the time. That is not how God wants us to live.

Sticking with the subject of wills for a moment, imagine if someone left you an expensive computer. If you're anything like me, then it won't be long before you're on the phone to a techy friend to ask for help on how to use it! Leaving such an item would be useless, unless you also left the instructions to go with it. Again, Jesus doesn't let us down. Not only does He leave us peace, but He tells us how to get it.

I think there are two main points here. Firstly, we must not let our hearts be troubled (agitated or disturbed). The onus is on us. Whether we get agitated or not is ultimately a choice we make. When something goes wrong, like a flat tyre say, we can stamp our feet, and even kick the car, but it won't help. By doing that, we're letting the devil walk all over us. Instead, we must chose to be peaceful.

Secondly, we must not be fearful. Fear opens the door for the enemy in our lives. When we're afraid, we're certainly not at peace. We must stand against fear, trusting in God and His Word completely and choosing faith instead.

Prayer
Lord Jesus, You have given us a precious gift of peace. Please help us to take hold of it each day. In Your name we pray, Amen

Questions to ponder or discuss:
- Would you describe yourself as a peaceful person?
- How can you be more peaceful? What can you do to increase your peace?

A Word of Encouragement – *Jesus came and died to give us peace, it must be pretty important! Seek peace today.*

Part 4 – Jesus' Teaching

Day 20 - Just do it!

"His mother said to the servants, Whatever He says to you, do it." - John 2:5 (Amp)

As we look at Jesus' teaching, we start with a verse from John. Today's verse comes from the account of Jesus turning water into wine at the wedding at Cana. Mary captures something so powerful, and yet so simple. She says, "Do what He tells you to do."

As we think about the Lord's teaching, we need to bear this simple instruction in mind. Obedience is the key to changing our lives. It's not enough just to know what Jesus has taught us; we must make every effort to do it as well. We live in an age where you can carry a hundred sermons around in your pocket on an MP3 player, where you can watch Gospel teaching on the television or Internet at any time, and where you can read countless books and Bible studies on any topic you might imagine. We have more knowledge than ever before, but not more obedience.

Jesus said that our obedience is directly related to how much we love Him (John 14:15, 23). The hard truth is that if we don't obey what God is telling us to do, then we don't really love Him. It is very easy to say that we love Jesus, because words don't cost all that much. However, when it comes down to obeying what He asks us to do, that can be quite difficult. I can say that I love God, but that means very little if I'm not willing to give up something He wants me to, or to be nice to someone He's put on my heart.

Sometimes we believe that God is an angry parent punishing us – this is never the case. God's anger was spent at the cross. When God is asking us to do something, whether that's giving something up or doing something difficult, He is not taking anything away. God is never trying to deprive you. In all He asks of us, He is trying to do good to us.

While obedience is connected to our love for God, I also believe it is connected to our level of maturity. If you know of a particularly blessed Christian, I strongly believe you will find that they are also an obedient Christian.

If you are not sure whether something is from God or not, first check with His Word. God will never contradict it, so if it doesn't line up, it's not from Him.

Questions to ponder or discuss:
- Why is it so hard to obey sometimes?
- What is God asking you to do?
- HOW CAN YOU SUPPORT SOMEONE AT CHURCH TO OBEY GOD?

A Word of Encouragement – *God wants to bless you with good things. It may be hard to obey, but it is best in the long run.*

Day 21 - Love your enemy

"But now I tell you: love your enemies and pray for those who persecute you." - Matthew 5:44 (Good news)

Has Jesus given us a more difficult command than this one? I'm not sure. It flies in the face of every natural (or should I say carnal) instinct we have. If someone does us wrong, we want to pay them back!

Yet Jesus teaches us to do something entirely different – something that is totally alien. Instead of paying our enemies back, He tells us to love them – *love* them! A million thoughts come up in our minds when we hear this – "But they don't deserve it!" "But they hurt me so badly!" "But it's just not fair!" "But... but... but..." All of these may be quite true, and yet Jesus' command could not be simpler – love them.

Why would Jesus ask us to do something so difficult? In my view, He asks us this because He wants us to live "shocking" lives. Jesus wants us, His people, to stand out in the crowd in such radical ways that people can't help but wonder at why we act the way we do. Now don't get me wrong, I don't mean you need to be radical with blue hair or living like a naturist, but rather you need to live out radical love. Jesus wants us to stand out because of our love – He wants people to be shocked by how much we love them.

I don't know if you have a great number of enemies in your life, but there are certainly those who have hurt you in one way or another I'm sure. These are the ones Jesus wants you to love. Do they deserve to be loved after what they've done? Probably not, but then, all of us have fallen short in some way. Did they hurt you? If so, then hurting them back won't in any way heal you. Is it fair that they receive love after what they've done? What about justice? Justice is not ours to give, but it is God's. I want to assure you that you will have justice. No one can escape the justice of our God, for we will all stand before Him one day.

Loving your enemies is a tough thing to do, but nothing will hurt you more than bitterness, anger and revenge. Let God work out your justice, and do what He tells you to do. Love those that hurt you – decide today to stand out from the crowd!

Prayer
Father, while we may not have enemies as such, we have plenty of people who've hurt us. Please help us to love them like close friends. In Jesus' name, Amen

Questions to ponder or discuss:
- Why do you think God wants us to love our enemies?
- What practical ways can you think of to love an "enemy" in your life?
- Are there people who have hurt you, who you can pray for right now?

A Word of Encouragement – *God deals with those who hurt His children, so don't waste your time trying to pay them back. Let God be God, and trust Him with everything.*

Day 22 - Giving

"Give, and it will be given to you. Good measure, pressed down, shaken together, running over, will be put into your lap. For with the measure you use it will be measured back to you." - Luke 6:38 (ESV)

Giving is a clear and huge part of Jesus' teaching, and it's important we learn to be "givers". A Christian who does not give, is like a Christian who does not pray.

Often preachers avoid the subject of giving because they worry people will think they are only after their money. While it is true that there are some false teachers who attempt to gain wealth by exploiting believers, there are also genuine teachers who want to share a vital teaching. What you must remember is this: God is never trying to take anything away from you, He's always trying to get you into a position where He can give you more.

Today's verse sets out clear benefits to the believer who will give – it will be given back to them, a good measure that is pressed down and shaken together. We all want to be blessed by God, but the size of the blessing He can give is entirely dependent on the "measure" we use. If we come to Him with an egg-cup, He can only give us an egg-cup's worth of blessing. If we come with a skip, then He can give us a skip-load of blessing! This "measure" is the size and attitude of our offering.

I believe God wants to prosper His people. Many disagree with something called the "prosperity Gospel" and that is a personal decision. My view is simply this: I want to bless my children with everything they are mature enough to handle, and God is a better Father than I am, so wouldn't He want that too?

We're not blessed for our own sake, and we need to remember that. We are blessed so we can be a blessing. God doesn't want us wallowing in our luxurious wealth, He wants us to use it to help those in need. That's why giving is so important. When you give to the church, or to a ministry, or to someone in need, you are promoting God's Kingdom. We should aim to give as much as we can to those in need, and God will take care of our needs Himself. And remember, God would rather us give a small gift with a good attitude, than a big gift with a terrible one. Be a cheerful giver!

Prayer

Father, thank You for today's verse which says You will give back to us in good measure. May you bless us, that we may be a blessing. In Jesus' name, Amen

Questions to ponder or discuss:
- Do you find giving difficult?
- Is money the only thing we can give?
- What needs can you meet in the lives of people you know?

A Word of Encouragement – *"Bring the full...tithes to the Temple... Put me to the test and ...I will...pour out on you in abundance all kinds of good things."* Malachi 3:10

Day 23 - Fasting

"And when you fast, don' t make it obvious, as the hypocrites do, for they try to look miserable and dishevelled so people will admire them for their fasting. I tell you the truth, that is the only reward they will ever get. " - Matthew 6:16 (NLT)

Fasting is something we don't always talk about, but is an important aspect of Jesus' teaching. As Jesus begins to discuss it, He says *"when you fast"* and not *"if you fast,"* so you can see that it is something He expects all of us to do.

If you've never fasted, or aren't even sure what it is – don't worry! Fasting, like prayer, is something we grow into. When you first start to pray, you may only pray the odd prayer here and there, and you may not be too confident doing it. But, as you learn more, you get more comfortable with it and soon it becomes an important part of your life. Fasting is just the same.

Fasting simply means to give something up for a time, usually food (but it doesn't have to be). You can fast for any period you feel led to, but if you're starting out, I'd suggest something like a four-hour fast (if you're giving up food that is!). Most of us can go without food for that long without any trouble. However, if you have any kind of medical condition that might be affected, please talk to your doctor first.

Some people fast regularly, some less often. Some fast for longer periods, while others do it over a shorter timescale. Some give up food or alcohol, and others the TV. The important thing is that whatever you give up, it should mean something to you. If you give up something you hate, then what's the point? If it doesn't move you, then it certainly won't move God.

Why do we fast? There are a number of reasons. We fast to remind ourselves how good our lives truly are. Some in the world ate less this week, than you've had for one meal. Secondly, we should fast with a purpose. Use the time you gain from fasting to spend with God. If you've given up food, then use the time you would normally spend eating, seeking God in prayer or His Word. Fasting can allow God to work more powerfully in our lives, and can often bring a breakthrough where it's really needed.

Lastly, fasting can teach our "flesh" to be more reliant on God's Word than on the food we eat.

Questions to ponder or discuss:
- Do you think fasting could aid your spiritual life?
- What could you give up for a time that would mean a great deal to you?
- Are there other believers you can join with for support in fasting?

A Word of Encouragement – *If you don't feel led to fast, it's OK. Don't fast because you think it's a "spiritual" thing to do, do it because you want to please God.*

Day 24 - Going the extra mile

"If a soldier demands that you carry his gear for a mile, carry it two miles." - Matthew 5:41 (NLT)

At the time that Jesus spoke these words, the Roman Empire was in charge over Israel. It was fairly common practice for a Roman soldier to stop you on the street and demand that you help carry his gear for a mile. Now I don't know how likely it is that today, in the UK, you would be stopped by a soldier (Roman or otherwise) and be called upon to carry their equipment. So what is Jesus saying to us? How can we apply this teaching in our lives?

This verse is where we get the phrase "Going the extra mile," and I've often heard it in a work context. At my place of work, we often describe the top performing staff as having "gone the extra mile." But what does it mean? It means doing above and beyond what is required of us. It means not getting by with just enough, but doing the best we can.

Jesus wants us to live excellent lives; He wants us to live extraordinary ones. God is not impressed when we do only enough to get by, or compromise our morals or standards. We need to surprise the world around us by living a life that goes beyond the norm.

Is your experience of the world one that goes beyond your expectations? Personally I can say, not at all! Often when we buy something, or hire someone to do a job, we have to make sure the work or product is up to standard. So often we are given below-par service or are even ripped off by people taking advantage. That is not what God wants for His people. We may expect this from the world, but not from God's people.

In every area of your life, I encourage you to do more than just what is expected. Surprise people – give them something extra. Get to work early, stay after church to help clean up, or if you need to give someone a call, give them a visit instead. God is looking for those who are willing to step out in the name of love. Are you up for the challenge?

Prayer

Father God, thank You that You don't settle for "just enough".
Thank You that You're a God who goes the extra mile. Teach us to be
a people who do the same, and give us the strength to surprise and
impress those around us with love. In Jesus' name, Amen

Questions to ponder or discuss:
- In what area of your life can you go the extra mile?
- How can going the extra mile be a good witness for Jesus?
- What are the characteristics of a person who is willing to go that
little bit further?

A Word of Encouragement – *Going the extra mile may cost you a little*
time or effort, but the rewards are worth it! Think of the good you can
do for God's kingdom just by surprising someone in a good way today.

Day 25 - Thankfulness

"He threw himself at Jesus' feet and thanked him—and he was a Samaritan." - Luke 17:16 (NIV)

Today, I want to talk about thankfulness. From a very young age, most of us were taught to say "thank you" at appropriate times. It was drilled into us how important it is to say those two words, and even more so to mean them. Thankfulness isn't simply a social convention we try to stick to, it is an important attitude and one we need to develop in our spiritual lives.

Today's verse comes from a time when Jesus healed ten leprous men. Of those ten, only one turned back to thank Jesus for what He had done. The verse points out that this man was a Samaritan, and not even part of the Jewish nation (the very people Jesus had come for first). Jesus asked, "Did I not heal all ten men? So where are the other nine?" He expected them to be grateful, and He expects us to be too.

God has done so much for us, and we need to recognise that. Each day, His grace and love work in our lives and we must take time to be grateful. We have a tendency to complain about things; perhaps this is because we have things so good in our lives. We complain if anything goes wrong, or if we don't get our own way. Complaining can be very dangerous; just look at Israel's journey through the wilderness in Exodus and Numbers! No matter how bad things are, there is always something to be grateful for. If you're struggling financially, then you ought to be thankful you still have a home. If you're health is not good, you ought to be grateful it's not more serious... And if it is, then be grateful you know the Lord!

One way to tell if you are thanking God enough is to examine your prayer life. Are you spending at least half your time thanking and praising Him? Or, like me, are you humbled into realising that you spend most of your prayers asking God for more, and not thanking Him for what He's already provided? Our petition (asking for things) should never outweigh our praise.

Prayer

Father, we ask You for nothing today, as You have already given so much. We simply thank You for all that You have done and continue to do in our lives. In Jesus' name, Amen

Questions to ponder or discuss:
- Why is it important to be thankful?
- Are your prayers more full of praise or petition? Do they need to change?
- What three things are you most grateful for at the moment?

A Word of Encouragement – *It shouldn't be difficult to think of things to be thankful for, but in case you're struggling, have a look at your dinner plate, wardrobe, church or family photo album.*

Day 26 - A new command I give you

"A new command I give you: Love one another. As I have loved you, so you must love one another." - John 13:34 (NIV)

As we finish this section on Jesus' teaching, we come to the most important thing He shared. That we should love one another.

Jesus called this a new command, because the Old Testament tradition was very much based around justice – an eye for an eye. If you were wronged, then you had the right to wrong the one who hurt you. There was room for compassion and forgiveness, but it was a road seldom used. An eye for an eye was a limit, not a necessity.

Jesus, as He did in so many ways, came to turn things on their head. He came to tell us that love was the way He wanted us to live. Never more so than now has that been true, and nothing would improve the world we live in more than by increasing love. It says in Matthew 24:12, "Because of the increase of wickedness, the love of most will grow cold."

The world is a cold place and love can be a rare thing. Not so for us though, as we ought to make love our first priority. Many Christians seek a ministry that they can serve God in, and perhaps the greatest ministry there is, is the ministry of love. Everyone has the ability to love, and it can be offered at no cost. It is practical and makes a tremendous difference to those who receive it. Love is the most excellent way (1 Corinthians 12:31).

I honestly believe that if every Christian in the world lived a life of true love, then evangelism would become completely unnecessary. The world would see us doing good and pouring out grace, and there would be no need to invite people to church – they would come willingly.

You may not think you can change the world, or that your life matters that much. But what life is insignificant, if it is dedicated to love? You may not be able to change the world, but you can change it for someone. Changing the world for the better is indeed a big job, but we do it by one act of love at a time. Oceans are huge, but they're made up of individual drops. Love everyone you can.

Prayer
Heavenly Father, help us to love. Please let our lives shine with love, that we may be a blessing to those around us. In Jesus' name, Amen

Questions to ponder or discuss:
- Is loving people always easy?
- How do you love the unlovely?
- What practical acts of love can you do today? If you're in a house group, share what you're going to do.

A Word of Encouragement – *People are desperately hungry for love – you can feed them today! Love costs nothing, so are you willing to give?*

Part 5 – Resisting the devil

Day 27 - We have an enemy

" He [Jesus] replied, "I saw Satan fall like lightning from heaven. "
- Luke 10:18 (NIV)

Where you live is perhaps a really pleasant place most of the time, and you may be privileged to be part of a loving church. Of course, life has its problems, but in general, life is pretty good for many of us. That being the case, it can be easy to forget that we have an enemy. It's not often we talk about the devil, but he is as real an enemy as you can imagine, and should not be underestimated.

Jesus said that He saw Satan fall like lightning from heaven. In the beginning, the devil was one of the angels and he worshipped God. But at some point, he decided that he wanted the worship for himself, and rebelled against God. The Bible tells us that he waged war against God and the angels, but of course was defeated. The devil was cast down from heaven, and now roams the earth.

In John 10:10, Jesus said that the devil comes only to steal, kill and destroy, and in John 8:44 it says "He [the devil] was a murderer from the beginning, not holding to the truth, for there is no truth in him. When he lies, he speaks his native language, for he is a liar and the father of lies." These verses alone paint a terrible picture of the devil's character, and we should remember his goal to destroy everything good that God has created.

The devil is real. He is a powerful force working in the world, and he will do what he can to disrupt your life as a Christian and the ministry of your church. We must be prepared to face him, and defend ourselves from his attacks. We'll spend the next few days looking at different ways to resist him.

Ephesians 6:16 talks about a shield of faith with which we can defend ourselves from the fiery arrows of the enemy. Paul also talks in 2 Corinthians 2 about us not being outwitted by Satan, and not being unaware of his schemes. I don't want you to be unaware, and I do want you to be ready to send the devil packing when he comes against you. I hope the coming days will give you an arsenal of weapons you can use against him.

Prayer

Father God, we know we have an enemy, but we also know that he is a defeated foe. You, Jesus, defeated him at the cross, and we ask that You will help us fight off his attacks when they come. In Jesus' name, Amen

Questions to ponder or discuss:
- Can you think of a time in your life when you were attacked by the enemy?
- Is it easy to see the work of the devil in the world today?
- What things do you think we can do as believers to fend off the devil?

A Word of Encouragement – *As believers, we have an enemy, but never forget that he is a defeated foe! Jesus has already won the victory!*

Day 28 - The Word is a weapon

"And take the helmet of salvation and the sword that the Spirit wields, which is the Word of God." - Ephesians 6:17 (Amp)

The Word of God (the Bible) is a spiritual weapon that we can use against the enemy. God's Word is living and active, and sharper than any two-edged sword (Hebrews 4:12). It is a powerful tool that we must employ when the devil attacks us.

In Matthew 4, we read the account of Jesus being tempted by the devil. It is an interesting encounter, and it demonstrates how we should respond when the devil attacks us. Three times the devil tempted Jesus, trying to get Him to disobey God. Firstly, he tempted Him to turn stones into bread (for He was hungry). Then, he tried to entice Him to leap from a tall building, so the angels would catch Him. Then finally, the devil offered Jesus all the kingdoms of the world, if He would worship Him.

Each time a temptation came, Jesus reacted in the same way. He said, "It is written..." and defeated the devil with God's Word. He spoke the Word out of His mouth, and put the devil in his place. We must do the same thing when temptation or attack comes against us. When the enemy comes, we send him packing with a verse of Scripture.

The devil tries to bring lies and deceit into our minds. He does this because if he can make you believe a lie, then he can stop you receiving and being all that God wants you to. How do we defeat those lies? With the truth of course! And the truth we use is the Bible.

2 Corinthians 10:4-5 says: "For the weapons of our warfare are not physical [weapons of flesh and blood], but they are mighty before God for the overthrow and destruction of strongholds, [Inasmuch as we] refute arguments and theories and reasonings and every proud and lofty thing that sets itself up against the [true] knowledge of God..." (Amp, underline added)

Get to know God's Word, and use it to defend yourself!

Prayer

Father, thank You for Your Word. Thank You that in this day and age, we have so much access to it in so many forms. May You help us use it to defeat the devil when he comes against us. In Jesus' name, Amen

Questions to ponder or discuss:
- Have you ever thought of God's Word as a sword or weapon before?
- Does the idea of speaking Bible verses out loud seem odd to you?
- What practical things can you do to help you get to know different verses better?

A Word of Encouragement – *Jesus said that you shall know the truth, and the truth will set you free. The Bible is our best source of truth in today's world!*

Day 29 - Justice against our adversary

" And there was a widow in that town who kept coming to him with the plea, 'Grant me justice against my adversary.' " - Luke 18:3 (NIV)

In Luke 18, Jesus tells the Parable of the Unjust Judge, which is sometimes called the Parable of the Persistent Widow. In this story, a widow comes to a judge and asks him to help her. However, because he was not a God-fearing man, he refused. She is not easily put off though, and continues to ask him over and over. Eventually, fed up with her constant request, he grants her justice.

Jesus tells us this story to illustrate that we should never give up in prayer. While this judge may be unjust, he grants her request, but God, who is full of love and compassion, will so much more grant the requests of His people when they are persistent in prayer.

When you read this story, you tend to focus on the two main characters – the judge and the widow. There is, however, a third character in this story who we may have missed – the adversary. The adversary is the one who is troubling the widow, and she needs the judge to intervene to give her justice.

We have an adversary, and he continually accuses and troubles us as well. In the same way as the widow, you and I need to seek God and ask for justice against that adversary. It is important we pray against the devil, and ask God to protect us and give us justice against him. The devil will always be there to attack and accuse us, so we must be equally persistent in our prayers against him.

Verse 8 of Luke 18 says, "I tell you, he [God] will see that they [His people] get justice, and quickly. However, when the Son of Man comes, will he find faith on the earth?" We need to be faithful for when Jesus returns, obeying His commands and dealing with the devil as we come into contact with him. If we do that, then God will answer our calls for help "quickly".

If you need to, cry out to God today and ask Him to give you justice!

Prayer
Lord God, we thank You that You are not like the unjust judge in Luke 18. Instead, You are full of grace and loving-kindness. Give us justice against our adversary the devil, so that we may serve You. In Jesus' name, Amen

Questions to ponder or discuss:
- In Matthew 6:7, Jesus tells us not to keep repeating words over and over again, what's the difference between that and being persistent in prayer?
- What does justice against the devil mean to you?

A Word of Encouragement – *Thank God that He is no unjust judge, but will grant our calls for justice quickly!*

Day 30 - The enemy attacks through people

"But he turned and said to Peter, "Get behind me, Satan! You are a hindrance to me. For you are not setting your mind on the things of God, but on the things of man." - Matthew 16:23 (ESV)

One of the most important things you can learn about resisting the devil is that he frequently attacks through people. If he is able to, he will attempt to steal your peace, tempt you and downright torment you through the people in your life. If he can, he'll use a Christian to do it, otherwise he'll use a non-believer to get to you.

Why does he do this? Firstly, he does it because people are all around you. Wherever you go, chances are there will be people there. It's a great conundrum because you can't love people if you're not around them, but if you are around them, then the devil has an opportunity to attack. Secondly, he attacks through people because we are God's creations and made in His image. If he can use people to cause trouble, then he thinks he can ruin God's creation.

Whether it is your spouse, child, boss or just the person in front of you in the Tesco queue, the devil will try to use them to tempt you to stop acting in a loving way. They may annoy you, insult you, disturb you or even abuse you, but you must remember that the devil is the problem, not the person.

In our verse for today, Jesus speaks rather harshly to Peter after he tells Jesus not to go to the cross. In reality, Jesus wasn't even talking to Peter, but to Satan working in him. "Get behind me!" Jesus cries, and we should learn to do the same. Now I'm not saying you should yell at people in Asda, calling them the devil! I am saying that we need to recognise when the enemy is attacking or hindering us, and tell him directly to get out of our way.

You can recognise when this is happening whenever you feel annoyed, irritated, offended or upset with someone. When those feelings come, say to yourself, "No, I'm not going to feel that way. This is just the devil trying to get me to lose control. I'm not doing it! Jesus died to give me peace, and I'm holding on to it!"

Questions to ponder or discuss:
- Does the above mean we should just let people treat us badly? (Hint – No!)
- Do you find it helpful to separate the devil from the person, when you've been upset?
- What can you do to keep your cool when someone annoys you?

A Word of Encouragement – *Anger is a natural response when we're treated badly, but use it to resist the enemy, and don't let it ruin your life or your witness!*

Day 31 - Shut Your Mouth!

"My God sent his angel, and he shut the mouths of the lions. They have not hurt me, because I was found innocent in his sight. Nor have I ever done any wrong before you, Your Majesty." - Daniel 6:22 (TNIV)

One of the ways that the devil tries to ruin your life, is by telling you lies. In John 8:44, Jesus describes the devil as being the "father of lies" and this is something we need to note. He may not speak to us with an audible voice, like you would talk to your friends or family, but he does speak. The lies he feeds us come into our minds; we hear thoughts like, "I'm no good," or "This is never going to work out." These lies can cripple us if we listen to them.

In 1 Peter 5:8, the Bible compares the enemy to a roaring lion. Our verse for today comes from the account of Daniel being thrown into the lion's den. That happened to Daniel because he refused to compromise his beliefs. The king was forced to throw him in with ravenous lions, and Daniel came out with not one scratch! This is because God sent an angel to shut the lion's mouths.

In a similar way, we need to pray that the devil's mouth will be tightly shut. When he feeds us lies about any subject – God's love for us, our friends or family, our forgiveness even – we should tell him directly to shut up! You are a child of God, and you don't have to put up with anything the enemy tries to do to you. When he lies, you need to call them what they are and tell him straight.

I want you to be clear that as long as you live on this Earth, Satan will never leave you alone. As long as you're serving God, and following Him, the enemy will try to stop you. He may fire a thousand lies at you a day, but you don't have to accept even one of them.

Thoughts are a little like birds – you can't stop them flying over your head, but you certainly don't have to let them build a nest in your hair either! Take captive every thought and make it obedient to Christ (2 Corinthians 10:5), and you will go a long way to stopping the devil from hindering your life.

Prayer
Dear Lord, help us to know the truth, and let that truth set us free.
We pray that the devil's mouth may be shut up tight, so that his lies
have no effect on us or our church. In Jesus' name, Amen

Questions to ponder or discuss:
- Do you often find yourself thinking negative thoughts?
- What can you do when one of the enemy's lies comes into your head?
- What does it mean to you to take every thought captive and make it obedient to Christ?

A Word of Encouragement – *You don't have to accept anything the devil gives you, shut his mouth and send him packing.*

Day 32 - Submit to God, resist the devil

"Submit yourselves, then, to God. Resist the devil, and he will flee from you." - James 4:7 (NIV)

We have spent a few days now talking about how to resist the devil. This is, I believe, an important subject and one we ought to think about from time to time. However, I don't want to spend any more time talking about the enemy – I'd rather talk about God!

The truth is that sometimes we can get so caught up fighting the devil, that we lose sight of Jesus altogether. The Lord is more important than anything else, and if we lose our focus – if the enemy steals it – then even by fighting him we can be playing right into his hands.

I've often heard Christians say, when they come under spiritual attack, "Resist the devil, and he'll flee!" Sadly, this is only a partial truth. A great many people quote this verse, or at least, part of this verse, and expect it to work. Resisting the devil only works when we are submitting to God first and foremost.

Your most effective weapon in spiritual warfare is to do exactly what God tells you to do. If the devil comes against you with people who are getting under your skin, then submit to God and love them. If the enemy tries to ruffle your feathers by delaying you in traffic, or by getting you stuck in a long queue; submit to God, and be patient. If Satan is stirring up strife in your church, then put a stop to it right then and there by being a peacemaker.

The strange truth is that the more we follow God, the more the enemy will want to try and stop us. However, the more we act the way God wants us to act, the less the devil's attempts to knock us off our stride will work.

If this whole idea of resisting the devil is new to you, or even a little uncomfortable, don't worry. My advice is seek God and follow Him with all of your heart. As you submit to Jesus as Lord, you'll learn to resist the enemy, and he will certainly flee from you!

Prayer
Lord, in all ways may we submit to You. As we do so, we trust You to take care of us and to help us keep the devil under our feet. In Jesus' Name, Amen

Questions to ponder or discuss:
- What does submitting to God mean to you?
- Do you find the idea of "submission" a difficult one?
- Do you think it's important to talk and learn about how to resist the devil?

A Word of Encouragement – *Don't worry about what the devil is doing, concentrate on what God is doing!*

Part 6 – Jesus' Ministry

Day 33 - Set the Captives Free

"He [Jesus] stood up to read...the book of...Isaiah. He⋯ found the place where it is written, 'The Spirit of the Lord is upon me, because he has chosen me to bring good news to the poor. He has sent me to proclaim liberty to the captives and recovery of sight to the blind, to set free the oppressed" - Luke 4:16-18 (Good News – edited for space)

As we near the end of our journey together, we start to consider Jesus' ministry. It's a ministry that we all look up to, and is the picture of what our ministries ought to look like. A quick read of any of the Gospels in the Bible, and you'll see that Jesus was followed by crowds of people. What did He do that attracted so many? And this was a time before newspapers, TV or Internet – why were people so intrigued by Jesus' work?

These few verses from Luke's Gospel give us a good idea of what Jesus came to do. We ought not to skim over these verses, as they are really important for us. So what do they tell us Jesus came to do? Firstly, Jesus came to bring good news. The Good News, or the Gospel message, is truly wonderful for us all. Jesus came to the Earth to save us from sin, and from an eternity apart from God. Jesus has bridged the gap between us and the Father, and while that meant eternal death, we now have eternal life through Him. That's good news indeed!

Secondly, these verses tell us that Jesus came to give sight to the blind. I believe this has two meanings. First of all, we see many occasions where Jesus actually restored vision to those who were blind. Jesus came to heal (which we'll talk about in a few days). But deeper than that, Jesus came to restore our spiritual eyesight. Many live in darkness, and don't even know it. Jesus came to give us eyes to see God.

Finally, Jesus came to set the captives free. Whether we're locked up in prison, or just trapped in a life of addiction, we need freeing. Perhaps you've never been locked in a cell, or trapped in a situation you couldn't get out of, but we've all ended up doing things we didn't want to do; hurting those we love or God Himself.

The Lord Jesus came to this planet so that we might be free – free from sin, or anything else that has trapped us. That is something to celebrate!

Questions to ponder or discuss:
- How has Jesus set you free?
- What does it mean to set captives free where you live?
- If the Gospel really is "Good News," then why do we find it difficult to share it?

A Word of Encouragement – W*hatever situation you find yourself in, Jesus can set you free! And whom the Son sets free, is free indeed!*

Day 34 - Jesus Stopped

"Jesus stopped and called them. "What do you want me to do for you?" he asked." - Matthew 20:32 (NIV)

This is a pretty unremarkable verse from Matthew's Gospel account – perhaps one you've read many times but that has never stood out to you. I want to draw your attention to it today, because I believe it contains a vital truth. This verse alone tells us a great deal about Jesus' ministry, and is something we could learn a lot from.

Jesus stopped.

Jesus was heading somewhere else; He was on a road and just happened upon someone who needed His help. And what did He do? He stopped. This is crucial, because it shows us that no matter what Jesus was doing, He always had time to stop for those who needed Him. We can learn a lot from this kind of attitude.

Today, you might be heading somewhere – maybe to work or school, maybe just to the shops. On your way, you might meet someone who needs your help, or you may get a call from someone who could use a hand. What will you do? Will you, like Jesus, stop? Or will you carry on with what you were planning on doing?

Our lives and ministries become both more powerful and more useful to God when we put them totally in His hands. It doesn't matter what your plan is for today, if you've consecrated (dedicated) your life to God, because if He needs you to do something else, you will do it.

Proverbs 16:9 says "A man's mind plans his way, but the Lord directs his steps and makes them sure." If you want to be like Jesus, then you have to be willing to set aside your plan for today, and be willing to be interrupted. Think of the Parable of the Good Samaritan (Luke 10:25-37), in that story there were "religious" people who refused to stop, and there was a Samaritan who did just that.

Are you going to "stop" today if need be?

Prayer
Jesus, You have led by example and shown us that when we see a need, we ought to stop and help out. May You give us strength to do just that today. In Your Name, Amen

Questions to ponder or discuss:
- Are you willing to give up your plans for today to "stop"?
- Why is it so difficult to stop and help sometimes?
- How can we make sure our eyes are open to the needs of those around us?

A Word of Encouragement – *What a man sows, he also reaps. Make sure you're sowing good seeds in case you need to reap assistance one day.*

Day 35 - Healed

"When evening came, they brought to Him many who were under the power of demons, and He drove out the spirits with a word and restored to health all who were sick." - Matthew 8:16 (Amp)

According to the Bible, Jesus spent a large amount of His ministry healing the sick. On the occasion above, we read that Jesus healed *all* who were sick. This is an amazing thing for us to grasp, as it is rare that we see such miracles. In my time, I can't remember many times when someone was healed in a miraculous way. I can certainly think of a number of times when God answered our prayers to heal and help unwell people, but as for what most would call a "miracle", they are less common than we would hope.

Is that the fault of God, or of us? If Jesus spent so much of His time ministering to the sick, He must have thought it quite important. And I believe it is no less important today.

In Hebrews 13:8, it says "Jesus Christ is the same yesterday and today and forever." If that is true, then Jesus is just as concerned about healing today as He was when He walked the Earth. If that's the case, why don't we see more people being healed?

There is no easy answer to that question, and we don't have time or space to go into it fully here. However, I do want to share a few points with you. Firstly, one reason we don't see more healing is that we often don't give God an opportunity. We run straight to the doctors (which you should do if you need to) and think of God as an afterthought. If we put Him first, then He can at least work with the doctors to improve our health.

Secondly, and I don't want to upset or offend anyone, but we are lazy. So many times do we pray a prayer of healing and just sit back waiting for God to do something. We don't understand He's already done it all! Half the time we don't even believe the prayer will be answered! I believe that if we want to be healed, we need to seek it. Look at the woman in Mark 5 who was healed of bleeding – she sought Jesus out and determined in her heart she was going to get to Him. We must do the same. Find out all you can about healing from

God's Word, and grab hold of Jesus with both hands!

Prayer
Lord Jesus, You spent a lot of time healing the sick, and we believe You still can and do now. Please teach us on this subject, and help us to seek You fully. In Your Name, Amen

Questions to ponder or discuss:
- Do you believe that God can and does heal today?
- Why do you think we don't see as many miracles as we would like in our church?
- How did Jesus heal people? Read Mark 5 for some ideas.

A Word of Encouragement – *Healing is a complex issue, but we must start by believing God is both willing and able to heal (Matthew 8:3)*

Day 36 - A Table for 5,000 Please

"They all ate and were satisfied, and the disciples picked up twelve basketfuls of broken pieces that were left over. The number of those who ate was about five thousand men, besides women and children."
- Matthew 14:20-21 (TNIV)

Have you ever had people round for dinner and you ended up with more guests than you were expecting? Even one or two extras can throw your plans out of the window! In our verses for today, we read about a time when Jesus and His disciples didn't just have one or two mouths to feed, but a whole lot more! The passage says there were 5,000 men in all, and that was besides the women and children. Some think there could have been as many as 20,000 people there that day!

You might want to read the whole story as it appears in Matthew 14, as there is a lot to focus on. I can imagine the colour draining from the disciples' faces when Jesus said in verse 16, "You give them something to eat." I'm not sure what I would have said in that situation; especially as there were no take aways in the area! It's an important lesson for us to learn. So often we ask God to do something, when really He's waiting for us to do it. "Lord, help so-and-so" we say, when He's waiting for us to help them ourselves.

There are three things I want to point out from the account of the Feeding of the 5,000. Firstly, we need to give Jesus what we've got. This miracle happened because someone gave Jesus their packed lunch. When they put their five loaves and two fish in a bag that morning, they probably had no idea what it would turn into. We need to give Jesus what we have and see what He does with it – even if we think it insignificant.

Another thing we must learn is thankfulness. Jesus, before He shared the food out, gave thanks to His Father for what He had provided. How thankful would you have been for a small lunch shared between so many? Nothing is too small to be grateful for.

Finally I want to point out the importance of fragments. Before they were done, Jesus told His disciples to collect the fragments that were left over, and they amounted to twelve basketfuls! In our wasteful society, we often forget how many small things make a big impact. Whether the fragments are coins, compliments or prayers, they soon add up to something greater. Don't neglect the fragments in your day today!

Prayer
Father, thank You for what You provide. As we bring to You even the smallest part of our lives, may You turn them into something that will bring You glory. In Jesus' Name, Amen

Questions to ponder or discuss:
- Do we often ask God to do things that we could do ourselves?
- What can you offer God to use, no matter how small or insignificant?
- Do we spend more time asking God for more, or thanking Him for what we have?

A Word of Encouragement – *If you're feeling like a "leftover" today, remember that Jesus specifically told His disciples to collect every single one!*

Day 37 - Show and Tell

"Now when the sun was setting, all those who had any who were sick with various diseases brought them to him, and he laid his hands on every one of them and healed them... And he was preaching in the synagogues of Judea." - Luke 4:40, 44 (ESV)

Why do you think Jesus' ministry was so successful? On more than one occasion, Jesus spoke to vast crowds numbering thousands, and this before the time of 24-hour TV news and the Internet. What made Him so popular? What did He do that drew in such vast crowds? Were the people just more "spiritual" than the people living today?

Jesus was an amazing speaker, whose messages both challenged and entertained (Jesus was often pretty funny). Jesus met the people's needs by healing the sick and driving out demons. Jesus helped the poor, and obviously had to handle a fair amount of finances as He had one of the Twelve to look after the money (John 13:29). Jesus even attracted little children to Himself, which tells us a great deal about the kind of Man He was.

All of the above is true, but I believe one of the reasons Jesus' ministry was so successful was that He used a "show and tell" model. Jesus didn't just preach *about* the Kingdom of God, but He *showed* the Kingdom through His actions.

Jesus would travel from place to place, heal the sick and help the poor, then He would preach to them. We, as a church, could learn a great deal about evangelism by studying this "show and tell" technique.

Often we try to preach to people without giving them one single good reason why they should listen. Jesus never had that problem. People listened to what He had to say because He had gone out of His way to help them first. Neither did Jesus "just" help them, but He stayed around long enough to teach them how to live in freedom.

If we want to reach the people living in our area, we need to give them a reason to listen to our message. Maybe we won't go around healing the sick and driving out demons (but why not I wonder!), but we can certainly help them in many ways. When we do that, we won't need to invite them to church, they'll invite themselves!

Prayer
Heavenly Father, help us to give people a reason to listen to Your Good News. As we walk in love, may You draw people into Your family. In Jesus' Name, Amen

Questions to ponder or discuss:
- Do you think people are more receptive to the Gospel after an act of love?
- What practical things can we do to help those in our community?
- Evangelism is hard for us all, but what can you do personally to share the Gospel?

A Word of Encouragement – *The Good News is actually good news, so let's do what we can to share it with others.*

Day 38 - Bread, Wine and Betrayal

"When it was evening, Jesus and the twelve disciples sat down to eat. During the meal Jesus said, I tell you, one of you will betray me." - Matthew 26:20-21 (Good News)

We draw near to the end of our forty days together. Over the next three days (including today), we'll be thinking about the last days of Jesus' ministry. All the wonders of Jesus' time on Earth – healing, miracles, parables and goodness, yet His greatest work was still to come.

Jesus and His disciples sat around a table sharing a simple meal. Knowing His time had almost come, Jesus wanted to spend His last hours of freedom with His closest friends. Yet what should have been a time of closeness, was tinged with sadness, as He knew one of them would betray Him. Imagine the shock and disbelief as He told them. "Surely it isn't me?" they would say. Even Peter, the "rock", would break when that betrayal came and would deny even knowing the Lord. What an evening it must have been for Jesus.

Picture that scene; a group of friends having a last meal together. It would be a strong memory for all of them, over the coming days. The last time they got to talk to Jesus. It would be important to remember that time, all He said, and remember Him as He was.

For us, too, we need to remember Jesus – what He did for us. And to help us do that, He gave us the gift of Holy Communion. Like the disciples, we also share a simple meal of bread and wine, and we do it in remembrance of Him. Every time we eat that bread, and drink that cup, we ought to think about Jesus and His sacrifice.
Communion seems like a strange tradition to many people. Bread that represents His body, and wine that symbolizes His blood. When we eat that bread and drink that cup, we proclaim the Lord's death until He returns (1 Corinthians 11:26). We do it to partake of the cross – of His greatest ministry. We take part in Communion, to take part in that ministry, to take part in the salvation that has been given to us. Communion should never be taken lightly, but certainly with

thanksgiving.

Jesus is our Lord and Friend, let's remember what He did for us today.

Prayer
Thank You for the gift of Communion Lord Jesus. As we eat with one another, and those across the world, we remember You. Praise Your great Name, Amen

Questions to ponder or discuss:
- What would it have been like to sit around that table with Jesus that night?
- What does Holy Communion mean to you?
- What does it mean to "proclaim the Lord's death until He returns" ?

A Word of Encouragement – *Life can be hard sometimes but we believers have good reasons to be joyful – we have salvation! Jesus has a place for us in heaven!*

Day 39 - The Cross

"And they took Jesus and led [Him] away; so He went out, bearing His own cross, to the spot called The Place of the Skull--in Hebrew it is called Golgotha. There they crucified Him, and with Him two others-- one on either side and Jesus between them." - John 19:17-18 (Amp)

We have reached the focal point of Jesus' ministry and the very reason that He came to Earth as a Man. Today, we're thinking about the Cross.

As I've mentioned, we've looked at many aspects of Jesus' work on Earth. In the Gospels, we see Him heal the sick, raise the dead, perform miracles and calm storms. But those things, as great and wonderful as they are, pale in comparison to the work of the Cross.

A "standard" crucifixion was a terrible thing in itself. I don't wish to be too gruesome or graphic, but it's important we recognise the suffering of our Lord. He, like the two men beside Him, was nailed to a rugged, wooden cross through His wrists and ankles. The wood wouldn't have been smooth and varnished like the crosses in many churches, but it would have been rough and full of splinters. There they would hang for hours and hours, barely able to breathe, thirsty and in terrible agony.

As bad as that is on its own, it was worse for Jesus. Not only did He suffer all that the other two men did, but also the weight of the world was on His shoulders. Every sin that had ever, or would ever be committed, was placed on His back and the agony and shame became His and His alone. Worst of all, the Father – His Father – turned His face away, leaving Jesus totally alone.

Jesus died, unlike most crucifixion victims, not of suffocation, but of a broken heart (we know this because of the water and blood that flowed from His side). His heart gave out under the intense pressure of mine, and your, sin. Jesus took on *our* punishment, and He suffered and died that we might receive eternal life – that our fellowship with the Father would be restored.

I can think of nothing further to write except, "Thank You, Lord!"

Prayer
May we not take Your cross for granted today Lord, but remember with a full heart all that You suffered on our behalf. What more can we say but "thank You," Amen

Questions to ponder or discuss:
- Psalm 22 prophetically describes the cross, how does it make you feel?
- What does the cross mean to you? Does it move your heart?
- What can you do today to thank Jesus for what He did at the cross?

A Word of Encouragement – *While Jesus was dying on the cross, He was thinking of you.*

Day 40 - It Is Finished

"When Jesus had received the sour wine, He said, It is finished! And He bowed His head and gave up His spirit." - John 19:30 (Amp)

Jesus' words recorded above capture so much. They signalled the end of His earthly ministry, and the completion of His most difficult but vital work. The words, "It is finished!" mean for us that Jesus has bridged the gap between us and the Father. While we were once far off, because of our Lord, we now have free access to our God and Father. His completed work has washed away our sins, and given us blessings unspeakable and beyond measure. In every sense, the work to restore humanity was finished once and for all. Nothing more can be done - the cross has said it all.

Yet, in another sense, the story is still unfolding. While Jesus' work is done, our work remains and we must press on to its completion. For us, our work is to take the Good News of the Gospel and share it with as many as we are able. It's our job to glorify God in our corner of the world.

Over the last forty days, we've looked at God's love for each of us, who we are in Christ, staying strong in our faith, the teachings of Jesus, resisting the enemy and studying the ministry of Christ. All of these elements (and others) are needed if we are to fulfil the Great Commission (Matthew 28:16-20). We won't succeed unless we know how much God loves us, and unless we do what we need to do to stay strong. We won't make it without knowing how to resist Satan or without obeying the teaching of Jesus. We've barely scratched the surface in our time together and must press on to what's ahead.

I hope you have enjoyed reading this devotional, and that it has both encouraged and challenged you. I want you to know that you are part of a loving family in the global church, and that without you, we are incomplete. We may differ in age, background, experience or personality, but we have one important thing in common – we all want to follow our Risen Lord.

God bless you!

Prayer
Father, as we finish our journey, may You encourage us forward.
Please help us to tell the community we live in about the finished work
of Christ. In Jesus' Name, Amen

Questions to ponder or discuss:
- What do the words, "It is finished!" mean to you?
- What has most challenged you over the last forty days, and what will you do about it?
- How can we support each other in telling people about Jesus?

A Word of Encouragement – *Jesus has finished the work, everything you need is found in Christ!*

About the Author

The best place to find out more about Andy is at his website:
www.andy-brown.org

Here you will find blog posts and audio teaching.

Andy is married to a wonderful wife, and is the father of four beautiful daughters.